THIS IS MY LONDON

BIS

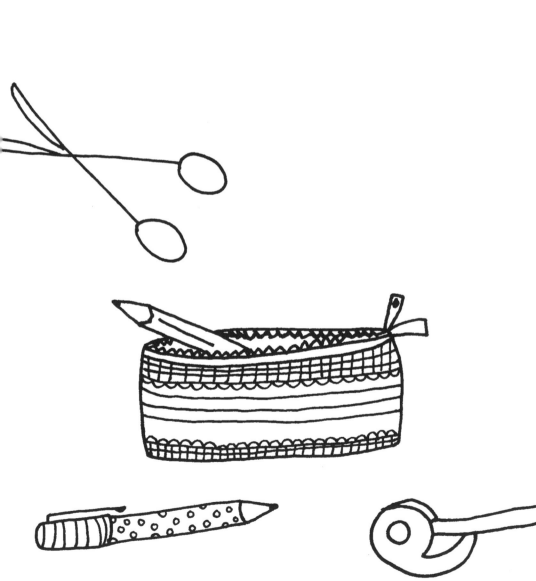

THIS BOOK BELONGS TO

DATE

I NEED TO GET TO KNOW
IT IN. EVERY QUIVER OF

LONDON AGAIN. BREATHE
ITS BEATING HEART.

SHERLOCK HOLMES

Things I would like to see and do in London

MARKERS, PENS, PENCILS & TUBES OF PAINT

CASS ART ISLINGTON
66-67 Colebrooke Row
London N1 8AB

ATLANTIS
Britannia House
68-80 Hanbury Street
London E1 5JL

AP FITZPATRICK
142 Cambridge Heath Road
London E1 5QJ

LONDON ART
132 Finchley Road
Hampstead
London NW3 5HS

L. CORNELISSEN & SON
105a Great Russell Street
London WC1B 3RY

JACKSON'S ART SUPPLIES HACKNEY
1 Farleigh Place
Stoke Newington
London N16 7SX

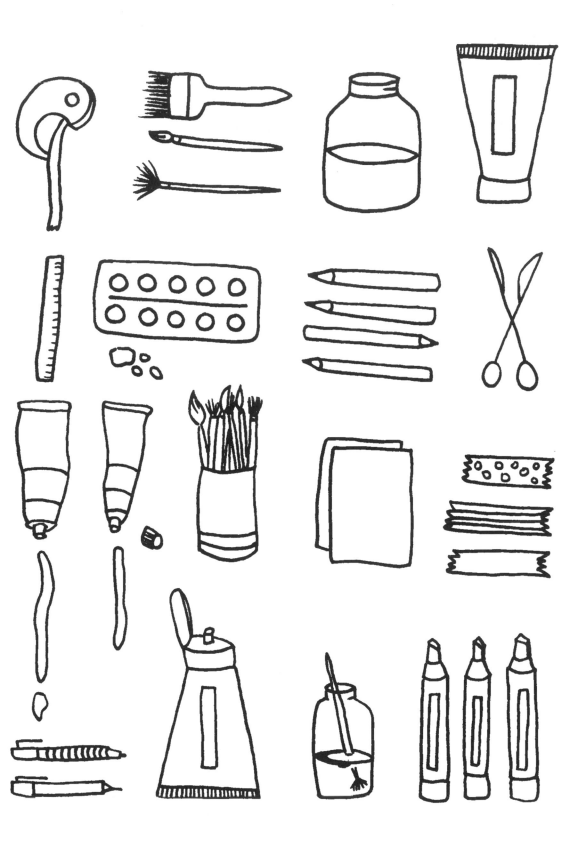

UNDERGROUND FOR PROS

Draw from the example of an actual Tube map: which London Underground have you taken, where did you get off, and what are the most beautiful names?

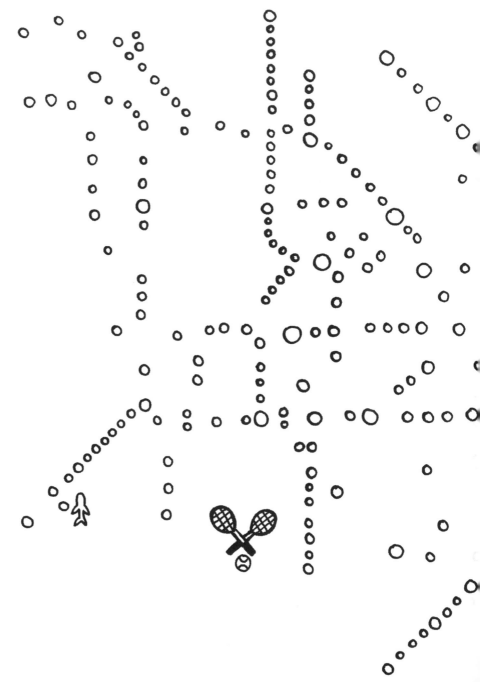

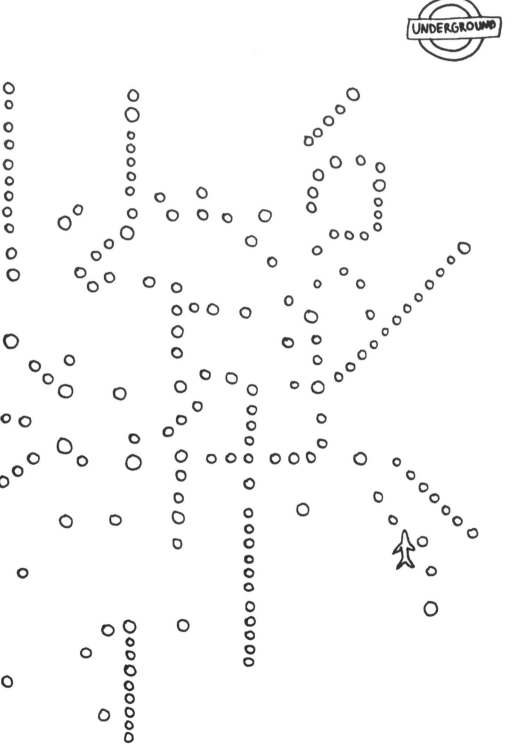

UNDERGROUND

COFFEE OR TEA, MY DEAR?

5X TRULY GREAT COFFEE

☐ **MONMOUTH COFFEE COVENT GARDEN**
27 Monmouth Street
Covent Garden
London WC2H 9EU

☐ **CARAVAN KING'S CROSS**
Granary Building
1 Granary Square
London N1C 4AA

☐ **ALLPRESS ESPRESSO ROASTERY CAFE**
58 Redchurch Street
Shoreditch
London E2 7DJ

☐ **PRUFROCK COFFEE**
23-25 Leather Lane
London EC1N 7TE

☐ **TOWPATH CAFÉ**
36 De Beauvoir Crescent
London N1 5SB

☐ ....
☐ ....
☐ ....

5X EXTRAORDINARY HIGH TEA

☐ **PRÊT-À-PORTEA**
The Berkeley (Hotel)
Wilton Place
Knightsbridge
London SW1X 7RL

☐ **MAD HATTER'S AFTERNOON TEA**
Sanderson London (Hotel)
50 Berners Street
London W1T 3NG

☐ **CLARIDGE'S**
49 Brook Street
Mayfair
London W1K 4HR

☐ **THE RITZ LONDON**
150 Piccadilly
London W1J 1BR

☐ **FORTNUM & MASON**
181 Piccadilly
London W1A 1ER

☐ ....
☐ ....
☐ ....

TICKETS &
BUSINESS
CARDS

Add your most beautiful ones to
this page, or copy them in a
drawing.

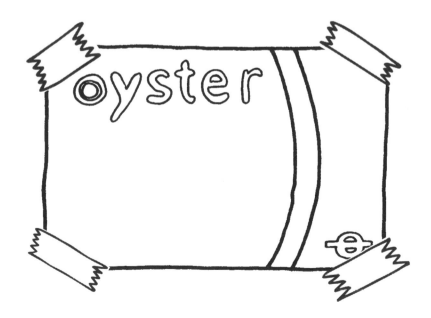

LONDON EYE

No matter where you are in the centre of London, you will be able to see the London Eye - up to the year 2000 also referred to as the Millennium Wheel - from truly any spot.

From the large Ferris wheel you can enjoy a splendid view (on a clear day up to a distance of 40 km away), but you do need to really want it: even with tickets bought in advance you face endless queues. When all capsules are full, you will be one of 800 passengers.

QUEEN ELIZABETH II

How many hats, crowns and scarfs do you think Queen Elizabeth II, born in 1926, has worn in her lifetime? She has been the queen since 1952, and there are countless photographs of her wearing countless kinds of headgear. Design a new one for her and colour the others.

SIGHTS YOU DO NOT WANT TO MISS

Obviously, you don't have to go, but these highlights are popular for a reason. Tick off the places you have visited. .

- ☐ ELIZABETH TOWER (BIG BEN)
- ☐ BUCKINGHAM PALACE
- ☐ PICCADILLY CIRCUS
- ☐ TOWER BRIDGE
- ☐ JEWEL TOWER
- ☐ HOUSES OF PARLIAMENT
- ☐ CANARY WHARF
- ☐ WESTMINSTER ABBEY
- ☐ ST PAUL'S CATHEDRAL
- ☐ TRAFALGAR SQUARE
- ☐ ROYAL ALBERT HALL
- ☐ DOWNING STREET 10
- ☐ DESIGN MUSEUM
- ☐ NOTTING HILL
- ☐ SOUTHWARK CATHEDRAL
- ☐ CITY HALL
- ☐ ....
- ☐ ....
- ☐ ....
- ☐ ....
- ☐ ....
- ☐ ....

FLOWERS, LEAVES & SHOPPING LISTS

Add your most beautiful finds to this page.

ETON MESS

Strawberries and cream; these two are inextricably linked to Wimbledon. Even tastier is Eton Mess, for which you add pieces of meringue to this desert. It has been served like that since the 19th century at the annual cricket games at Eton, the famous boarding school.

500 gr. strawberries
250 ml cream,
100 gr. thick pieces of meringue

Mash up half of the strawberries with a fork. Stir this purée carefully in with the cream and pieces of meringue. Divide into 6 cups or glasses and garnish with the rest of the strawberries.
Eat immediately!

4 egg whites
150 gr. powdered sugar
pinch of salt

If you want to make the meringue yourself: Preheat the oven at 50 °C. Add the egg white to a clean bowl. Beat until frothy, add the powdered sugar and the salt and beat until you can form stiff peaks from the egg whites. Divide into tufts on the baking tray covered with baking paper and place in the oven. Leave the egg white foam in the oven until it has dried completely (although slightly moist can also be tasty). This takes about 2 hours.

ELIZABETH TOWER

The clock tower at
The Palace of Westminster
built in 1858
334 steps

Yes, this tower is often referred to
as the Big Ben, but that is actually
not accurate. The truth is: the
tower was long referred to as the
Clock Tower until, upon Queen
Elizabeth's 60-year anniversary
in 2012, it was name after her:
Elizabeth Tower. The Big Ben does
exist, though: it is the great bell
hanging in the tower. The Palace
of Westminster is the building
from which the Houses or
Parliament govern the kingdom.

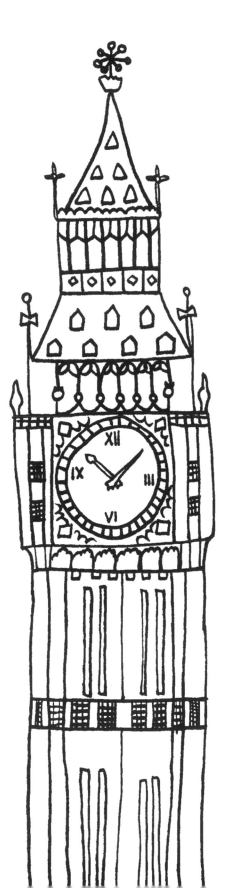

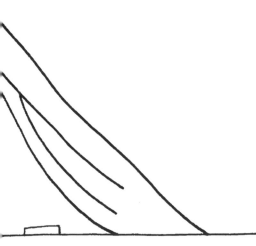

BRING ON THE NIGHT ...

IN THE PUB YOU DRINK BEER, FULL STOP.
HAVE YOU ORDERED SOMETHING ELSE ANYWAY?

☐ G&T

☐ PALE ALE

☐ PIMM'S

☐ WODKA MARTINI

☐ ELDERFLOWER CORDIAL

☐ DAISY

☐ CIDER

☐ SIDECAR

☐ ....

☐ ....

☐ ....

RULES FOR IN THE PUB

☐ ALWAYS-ALWAYS-ALWAYS ORDER AT THE BAR

☐ GET A ROUND FOR THE WHOLE GROUP; IT IS *NOT DONE* TO EACH ORDER YOUR OWN

☐ DRINK BEER. ONE DOES NOT DRINK COCKTAILS IN THE PUB.

☐ PLACE YOUR ORDER QUICKLY, AS IF YOU HAVE BEEN COMING HERE FOR YEARS AND DO SO DAILY

☐ BE GENEROUS: BUYING ROUNDS IS HOW IT'S DONE.

☐ ....

5X BEAUTIFUL OLD-FASHIONED PUB

☐ YE OLDE CHESIRE CHEESE
   145 Fleet Street, London EC4A 2BU

☐ PRINCESS LOUISE
   208 High Holborn, London, WC1V 7EP

☐ KING'S HEAD
   115 Upper Street, Islington, London N1 1QN

☐ SOUTHAMPTON ARMS
   139 Highgate Road, London NW5 1LE

☐ THE SPURSTOWE ARMS
   68 Greenwood Road, London E8 1AB

☐ ....

LONDON BOROUGHS

Colour the districts you have
visited, the ones you still wish to
visit, or where you would purchase
a pied-à-terre if you won the
lottery.

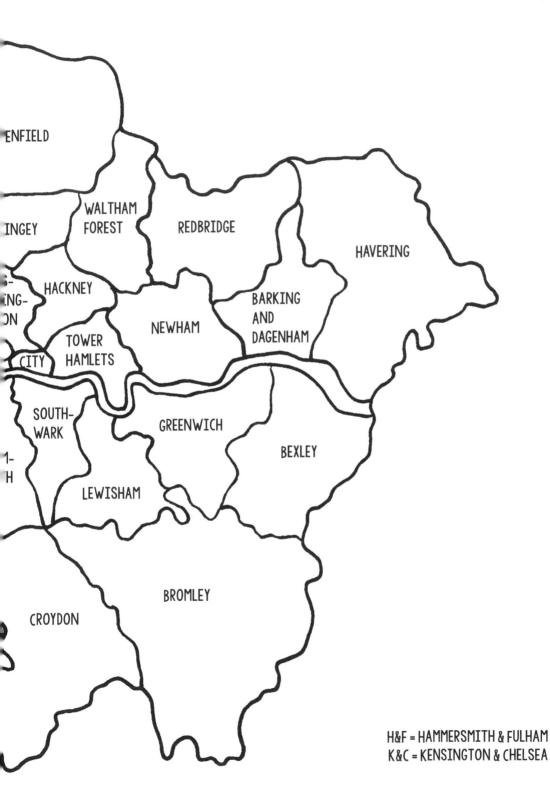

ENFIELD

INGEY

WALTHAM
FOREST

REDBRIDGE

HAVERING

HACKNEY

ING-
ON

NEWHAM

BARKING
AND
DAGENHAM

TOWER
HAMLETS

CITY

SOUTH-
WARK

GREENWICH

BEXLEY

I-
H

LEWISHAM

BROMLEY

CROYDON

H&F = HAMMERSMITH & FULHAM
K&C = KENSINGTON & CHELSEA

Dreams, notes, ideas, discoveries

GALLERIES & MUSEUMS

Of course, these types of lists could go on and on, as London has a wealth of splendid museums and galleries. In case of choice overload, make sure to visit one or more of these ten addresses to ensure that you have at least seen some of the best-known ones.

GALLERIES

☐ SAATCHI GALLERY
   www.saatchigallery.com

☐ WHITECHAPEL GALLERY
   www.whitechapelgallery.org

☐ HOXTON ART PROJECTS
   www.hoxtonartprojects.com

☐ SERPENTINE GALLERY
   www.serpentinegalleries.org

☐ ....

☐ ....

☐ ....

☐ ....

☐ ....

MUSEUMS

☐ VICTORIA & ALBERT MUSEUM
   www.vam.ac.uk

☐ TATE MODERN
   www.tate.org.uk

☐ SCIENCE MUSEUM
   www.sciencemuseum.org.uk

☐ NATIONAL PORTRAIT GALLERY
   www.npg.org.uk

☐ DESIGN MUSEUM
   www.designmuseum.org

☐ BRITISH MUSEUM
   www.britishmuseum.org

☐ ....

☐ ....

☐ ....

☐ ....

☐ ....

DOWNING STREET 10

By far the most famous residence in London, Downing Street 10 is the home of the prime minister. The front door looks pretty normal, but the house is actually a bunker. The man whom we put next to the front door on this page does not live here and is also not planning to any time soon. It is Boris Johnson, London's current eccentric mayor. It was he who once spoke the legendary words: 'My chances of being PM are about as good as the chances of finding Elvis on Mars, or my being reincarnated as an olive.'

TAKEAWAY & STREET FOOD

In London you can enjoy really good food: fantastic restaurants, gastropubs and many fun places to dine. And let's not forget the street food markets, food trucks and other stalls, trendy fish 'n' chips places and much more.

WHERE?

- [ ] POPPIES
  www.poppiesfishandchips.co.uk

- [ ] STREET KITCHEN (FOOD TRUCKS)
  www.streetkitchen.co.uk

- [ ] KERB
  www.kerbfood.com

- [ ] STREET FEAST
  www.streetfeastlondon.com

- [ ] URBAN FOOD FEST
  www.urbanfoodfest.com

- [ ] BROCKLEY MARKET
  www.brockleymarket.com

- [ ] WAPPING MARKET
  www.wappingmarket.com

- [ ] BERWICK STREET
  www.berwickstreetlondon.co.uk

- [ ] ....

WHAT?

- [ ] FISH 'N' CHIPS
- [ ] INDIAN CURRY
- [ ] PORK PIE
- [ ] SCOTCH EGG
- [ ] CHURROS
- [ ] BURGERS
- [ ] PULLED PORK SANDWICH
- [ ] BURRITOS

- [ ]

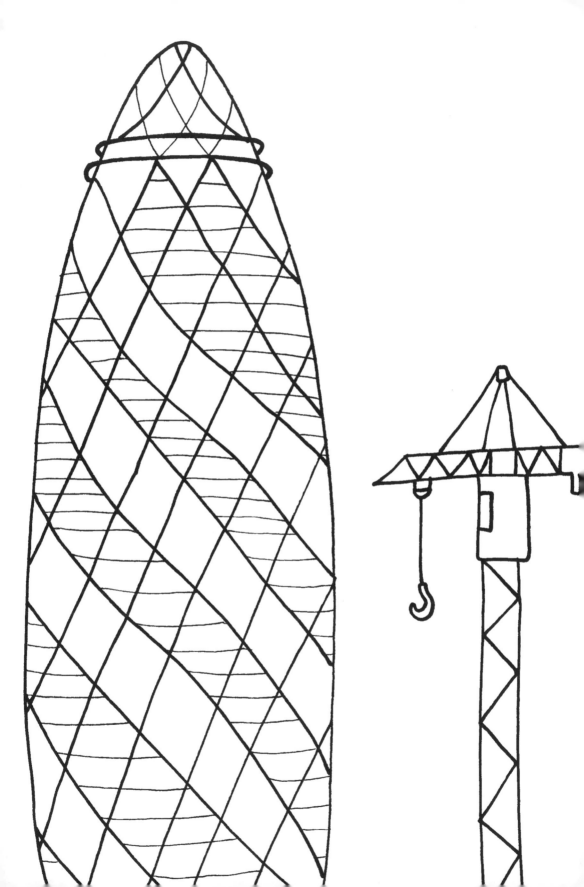

THE GHERKIN

Are there any buildings in London that do not have a nickname? The Gherkin is actually called 30 St Mary Axe, but of course The Gherkin is such a better name. And easier to remember. The building (180 metres in height, opened in 2004) was designed by Sir Norman Foster and is used as an office building in the heart of the City. Its aerodynamic shape ensures less wind turbulence around it, and the building is the fifth tallest building in the city. It is claimed to be the first 'ecological skyscraper in the world'. You cannot enter it, unless you work here or were invited to a party on the top floor.

TO THE MARKET

Yes, the London markets are famous. Some are fully dedicated to provisions and food, others offer vintage clothing and interior decoration accessories. Perfect day out on the weekend!

☐ **SUNDAY UPMARKET**
Ely's Yard, The Old Truman Brewery
London E1 6QL
www.sundayupmarket.co.uk

☐ **BOROUGH MARKET**
Southwark Street, London SE1 1TL
boroughmarket.org.uk

☐ **MALTBY STREET MARKET**
The Ropewalk, Maltby Street
London SE1 2HQ
www.maltby.st

☐ **PORTOBELLO ROAD MARKET**
Portobello Road, London W10 5TA
www.portobelloroad.co.uk

☐ **BROADWAY MARKET**
Broadway Market, London E8
www.broadwaymarket.co.uk

☐ **SPITALFIELDS MARKET**
Brushfield Street, London E1 6AA
www.spitalfields.co.uk

☐ **CHATSWORTH ROAD MARKET**
Chatsworth Road, London E5
www.chatsworthroade5.co.uk/market/

☐ **SMITHFIELD MARKET**
London Central Markets, London EC1A 9PS
www.smithfieldmarket.com

(NOT) ON THE HIGH STREET

Yes, you definitely need to pay a visit to the large, well-known department stores in London. But there is more, as the city offers lots of special flagship stores, such as these!

FLAGSHIP STORES

☐ **URBAN OUTFITTERS**
200 Oxford Street
London W1D 1NU

☐ **ANTHROPOLOGIE**
158 Regent Street
London W1B 5SW

☐ **THE CONRAN SHOP**
Michelin House
81 Fulham Road
London SW3 6RD

☐ **PAUL SMITH**
9 Albemarle Street
London W1S 4BL

☐ ....
☐ ....
☐ ....

DEPARTMENT STORES

☐ **LIBERTY LONDON**
Regent Street / Great Marlborough Street
London W1B 5AH

☐ **SELFRIDGES & CO**
400 Oxford Street
London W1A 1AB

☐ **HARRODS**
87-135 Brompton Road
London SW1X 7XL

☐ **JOHN LEWIS**
300 Oxford Street
London W1C 1DX

☐ **FORTNUM & MASON**
181 Piccadilly
London W1A 1ER

☐ **HARVEY NICHOLS**
109-125 Knightsbridge
London SW1X 7RJ

☐ ....
☐ ....
☐ ....

FILMS IN, ABOUT & FROM LONDON

☐ LOCK, STOCK & TWO SMOKING BARRELS

☐ BRIDGET JONES'S DIARY

☐ FOUR WEDDINGS AND A FUNERAL

☐ CLOSER

☐ SKYFALL

☐ LOVE ACTUALLY

☐ THE KING'S SPEECH

☐ A FISH CALLED WANDA

☐ NOTTING HILL

☐ SHERLOCK HOLMES

☐ HARRY POTTER AND THE PHILOSOPHER'S STONE

☐ SHAKESPEARE IN LOVE

☐ SWEENEY TODD, THE DEMON BARBER OF FLEET STREET

☐ ....

☐ ....

☐ ....

BORN IN LONDON!

- ☐ AMY WINEHOUSE
- ☐ THE CLASH
- ☐ COLDPLAY
- ☐ PET SHOP BOYS
- ☐ THE ROLLING STONES
- ☐ ROD STEWART
- ☐ SEX PISTOLS
- ☐ THE XX
- ☐ UNKLE
- ☐ ADELE
- ☐ LED ZEPPELIN
- ☐ ....
- ☐ ....
- ☐ ....

25.000 BLACK CABS

Black Cabs, the well-known London taxis, can truly be spotted all over the city. They used to all be black, but nowadays they come in other colours, too. Make it your best work.

MIND THE GAP!

At which stops did you get off? Highlight them here!

Acton Town
Aldgate
Aldgate East
All Saints
Alperton
Amersham
Angel
Archway
Arnos Grove
Arsenal
Baker Street
Balham
Bank
Barbican
Barking
Barkingside
Barons Court
Bayswater
Beckton
Beckton Park
Becontree
Belsize Park
Bermondsey
Bethnal Green
Blackfriars
Blackhorse Road
Blackwall
Bond Street
Borough
Boston Manor
Bounds Green
Bow Church
Bow Road
Brent Cross
Brixton
Bromley-by-Bow
Buckhurst Hill
Burnt Oak
Caledonian Road
Camden Town
Canada Water
Canary Wharf
Canning Town
Cannon Street
Canons Park
Chalfont & Latimer
Chalk Farm
Chancery Lane

Charing Cross
Chesham
Chigwell
Chiswick Park
Chorleywood
Clapham Common
Clapham North
Clapham South
Cockfosters
Colindale
Colliers Wood
Covent Garden
Crossharbour & London
Arena
Croxley
Custom House
Cutty Sark for Maritime
Greenwich
Cyprus
Dagenham East
Dagenham Heathway
Debden
Deptford Bridge
Devons Road
Dollis Hill
Ealing Broadway
Ealing Common
Earl's Court
East Acton
East Finchley
East Ham
East India
East Putney
Eastcote
Edgware
Edgware Road
Elephant & Castle
Elm Park
Elverson Road
Embankment
Epping
Euston
Euston Square
Fairlop
Farringdon
Finchley Central
Finchley Road
Finsbury Park

Fulham Broadway
Gallions Reach
Gants Hill
Gloucester Road
Golders Green
Goldhawk Road
Goodge Street
Grange Hill
Great Portland Street
Green Park
Greenford
Greenwich
Gunnersbury
Hainault
Hammersmith
Hampstead
Hanger Lane
Harlesden
Harrow & Wealdstone
Harrow-on-the-Hill
Hatton Cross
Heathrow 1,2,3
Heathrow 4
Heathrow 5
Hendon Central
Héron Quays
High Barnet
High Street Kensington
Highbury & Islington
Highgate
Hillingdon
Holborn
Holland Park
Holloway Road
Hornchurch
Hounslow Central
Hounslow East
Hounslow West
Hyde Park Corner
Ickenham
Island Gardens
Kennington
Kensal Green
Kensington
Kentish Town
Kenton
Kew Gardens
Kilburn

Kilburn Park
King George V
King's Cross St. Pancras
Kingsbury
Knightsbridge
Ladbroke Grove
Lambeth North
Lancaster Gate
Langdon Park
Latimer Road
Leicester Square
Lewisham
Leyton
Leytonstone
Limehouse
Liverpool Street
London Bridge
London City Airport
Loughton
Maida Vale
Manor House
Mansion House
Marble Arch
Marylebone
Mile End
Mill Hill East
Monument
Moor Park
Moorgate
Morden
Mornington Crescent
Mudchute
Neasden
New Cross
New Cross Gate
Newbury Park
North Acton
North Ealing
North Greenwich
North Harrow
North Wembley
Northfields
Northolt
Northwick Park
Northwood
Northwood Hills
Notting Hill Gate
Oakwood

Old Street	Royal Oak	Stonebridge Park	Waterloo
Osterley	Royal Victoria	Stratford	Watford
Oval	Ruislip	Sudbury Hill	Wembley Central
Oxford Circus	Ruislip Gardens	Sudbury Town	Wembley Park
Paddington	Ruislip Manor	Surrey Quays	West Acton
Park Royal	Russell Square	Swiss Cottage	West Brompton
Parsons Green	Seven Sisters	Temple	West Finchley
Perivale	Shadwell	Theydon Bois	West Ham
Piccadilly Circus	Shepherd's Bush	Tooting Bec	West Hampstead
Pimlico	Shepherd's Bush Market	Tooting Broadway	West Harrow
Pinner	Sloane Square	Tottenham Court Road	West India Quay
Plaistow	Snaresbrook	Tottenham Hale	West Kensington
Pontoon Dock	South Ealing	Totteridge and Whetstone	West Ruislip
Poplar	South Harrow	Tower Gateway	West Silvertown
Preston Road	South Kensington	Tower Hill	Westbourne Park
Prince Regent	South Kenton	Tufnell Park	Westferry
Pudding Mill Lane	South Quay	Turnham Green	Westminster
Putney Bridge	South Ruislip	Turnpike Lane	White City
Queen's Park	South Wimbledon	Upminster	Whitechapel
Queensbury	South Woodford	Upminster Bridge	Willlesden Green
Queensyway	Southfields	Upney	Willlesden Junction
Ravenscourt Park	Southgate	Upton Park	Wimbledon
Rayners Lane	Southwark	Uxbridge	Wimbledon Park
Redbridge	St. James's Park	Vauxhall	Wood Green
Regent's Park	St. John's Wood	Victoria	Wood Lane
Richmond	St. Paul's	Walthamstow	Woodford
Rickmansworth	Stamford Brook	Wanstead	Woodside Park
Roding Valley	Stanmore	Wapping	Woolwich Arsenal
Rotherhithe	Stepney Green	Warren Street	
Royal Albert	Stockwell	Warwick Avenue	

LONDON
CALLING

There are actually not so many
bright red phone booths left in
London, thanks to all the mobile
phones, of course. There were
once about 60,000 of them located
across the country. Now, only
10,000 remain. However, the Brits
are not able to entirely say farewell
to this icon. Some telephone
booths have been converted to
small libraries or galleries, others
have been adopted by the
municipality.

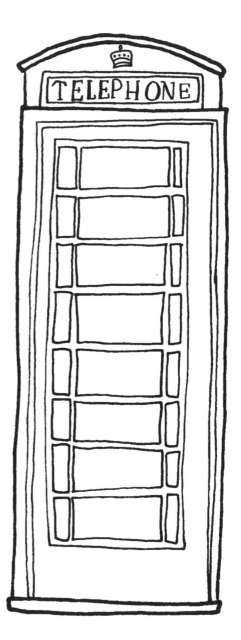

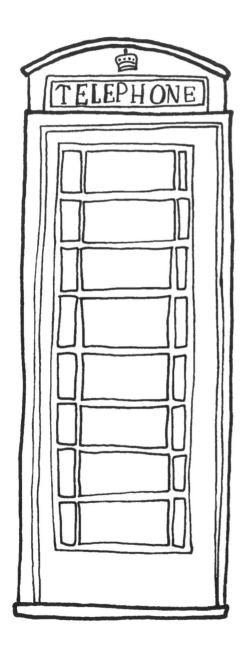
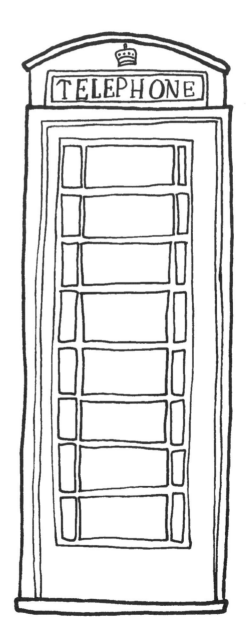

TODAY
WE DO
NOTHING!

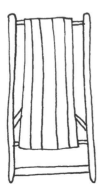
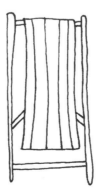

THEATRE & MUSICALS

"All the world's a stage" William Shakespeare once said. Still, the most beautiful stages can be found in London. Head to the West End for the well-known large theatres, or discover one of the smaller stages in other parts of the city.

☐ **THE OLD VIC**
    The Cut/Waterloo Road
    London SE1 8NB
    www.oldvictheatre.com

☐ **ROYAL OPERA HOUSE**
    Bow Street/Floral Street
    London WC2E 9DD
    www.roh.org.uk

☐ **THE NATIONAL THEATRE**
    Southbank/Upper Ground
    London SE1 9PX UK
    www.nationaltheatre.org.uk

☐ **SHAKESPEARE'S GLOBE**
    Bankside/21 New Globe Walk
    London SE1 9DT
    www.shakespearesglobe.com

☐ **SADLER'S WELLS THEATRE**
    Rosebery Avenue
    London EC1R 4TN
    www.sadlerswells.com

☐ ....

☐ ....

☐ ....

TOWER BRIDGE

Opened in 1894
Bridge across the River Thames
244 metres long,
65 metres in height
Opens approx. 850x per year

One of the most photographed and
visited sights of London, together
with the Elizabeth Tower (or the
Big Ben).. There is a permanent
exhibition under the bridge, which
is well worth a visit. A new feature
is the glass floor at the top of the
bridge: standing on it, you can stare
all the way down.

Spots I have visited and wish to remember

LOOK LEFT, LOOK RIGHT, LOOK BOTH SIDES

Crossing the street in London is an endeavour in its own right. Yes, there are traffic lights, but no, you must not in the least be distracted by them. Even if there are three police officers across the street, a Londoner will certainly walk through a red light once the coast is clear. Look Left, Look Right, Look Both Sides: always-always-always look more often than you deem necessary. The most famous pedestrian crossing in the city can be found at Abbey Road, where in 1969 The Beatles casually crossed the road for the cover of their new album.

THE FANTASTIC
MR FOX

You might just spot one out of
nowhere, in the middle of the street
and also in broad daylight: there are
thousands of foxes living in London.
It is unknown how many there are
exactly, as estimates run from 5,000
up to more than 30,000.

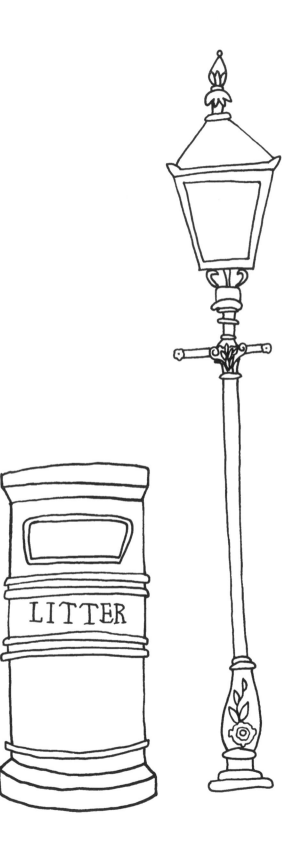

LITTER

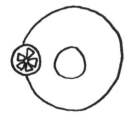

COME, LET US HAVE SOME TEA AND CONTINUE TO TALK ABOUT HAPPY THINGS

CHAIM POTOK

COME RAIN
OR SHINE

It's a great myth that it always rains
in London. The annual rainfall even
amounts to fewer millimetres than
in Amsterdam or Berlin. Of course,
the notion that Londoners always
look fashionable, come rain or
shine, is a fact indeed.

BEAUTIFUL BOOKSHOPS

☐ **PERSEPHONE BOOKS**
59 Lamb's Conduit Street
London WC1N 3NB

☐ **DAUNT BOOKS**
Multiple locations across the city
www.dauntbooks.co.uk

☐ **LONDON REVIEW BOOKSHOP**
14 Bury Place
London WC1A 2JL

☐ **FOYLES**
Multiple locations across the city
www.foyles.co.uk

☐ **JOHN SANDOE [BOOKS] LTD**
S10 Blacklands Terrace
London SW3 2SR

☐ **GOSH!**
1 Berwick Street
London W1F 0DR

☐ **HATCHARDS PICCADILLY**
187 Piccadilly
London W1J9LE

☐ **BOOKS FOR COOKS**
4 Blenheim Crescent
London W11 1NN

☐ ....

☐ ....

☐ ....

BOOKS ABOUT LONDON

☐ **SAM SELVON,** The Lonely Londoners

☐ **EVELYN WAUGH,** Vile Bodies

☐ **ALAN HOLLINGHURST,**
The Line of Beauty

☐ **TIM LOTT,** White City Blue

☐ **DAVID LODGE,**
The British Museum is Falling Down

☐ **MARTIN AMIS,** London Fields

☐ **NORMAN COLLINS,** London Belongs to Me

☐ **VIRGINIA WOOLF,** Mrs Dalloway

☐ **ALAN JOHNSON,**
This Boy: A Memoir of a Childhood

☐ **JULIAN BARNES,** Letters from London

☐ **RACHEL LICHTENSTEIN,** On Brick Lane

☐ **HANIF KUREISHI,** The Buddah of Suburbia

☐ **P.G WODEHOUSE,** The Jeeves Omnibus no.1

☐ ....

☐ ....

☐ ....

TALL PEOPLE, SHORT PEOPLE, FAT PEOPLE, SKINNY PEOPLE

Who is sitting across from you in the Underground? Draw them!

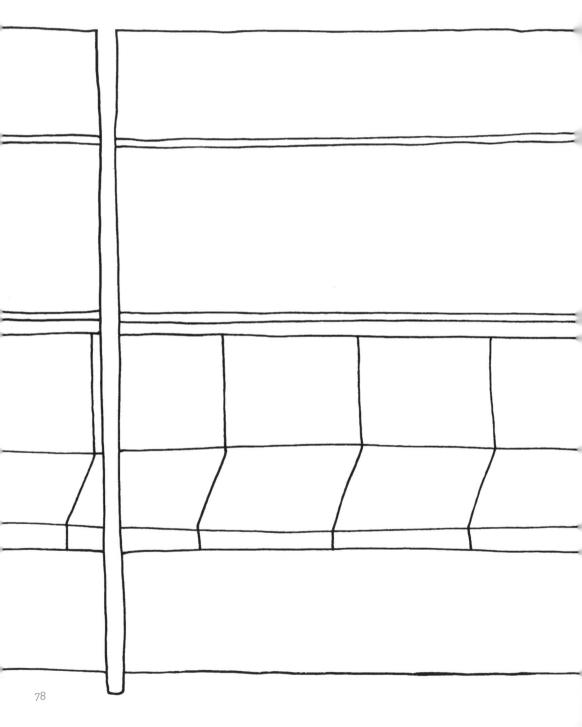

QUEEN'S GUARD

Don't: try to make one of the Royal
Guards - who, if they work at the
palace, are referred to as the Queen's
Guard - laugh. However, Do: help
these men change their style
completely.

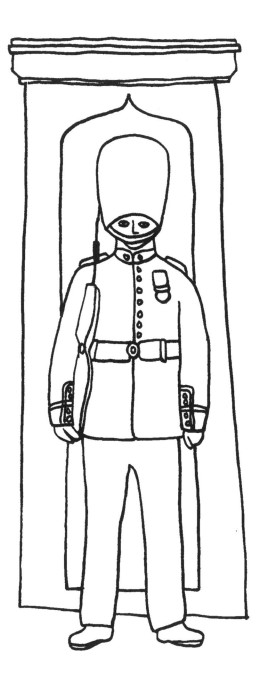

COCKNEY RHYMING SLANG

One of the most beautiful dialects in the world emerged at the end of the 19th century in the East End. For the Cockneys the explanation is very simple, but outsiders often have a hard time deciphering the broad English accent. This is the idea: the original word is replaced by a combination of two other words. 'Telephone' becomes 'dog' because telephone rhymes with dog-and-bone. That can (at times) get a bit lengthy, so you leave out the second part. Easy enough, right?

OXO CUBE
(TUBE)

MINCE PIES
(EYES)

ROSY
(TEA)

BETTER THAN A TEXT MESSAGE

Below, note down the names of five people, buy
five postcards and five stamps, and then write
five beautiful sentences on each card.
Do not forget to post.

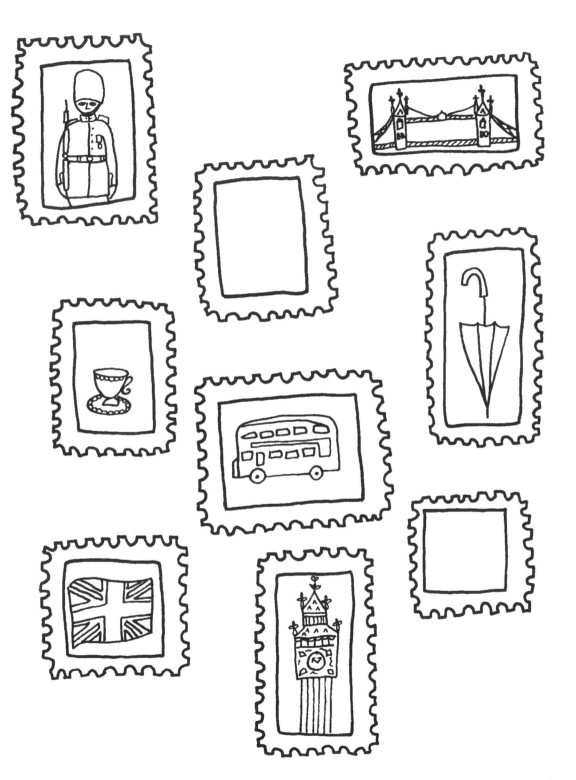

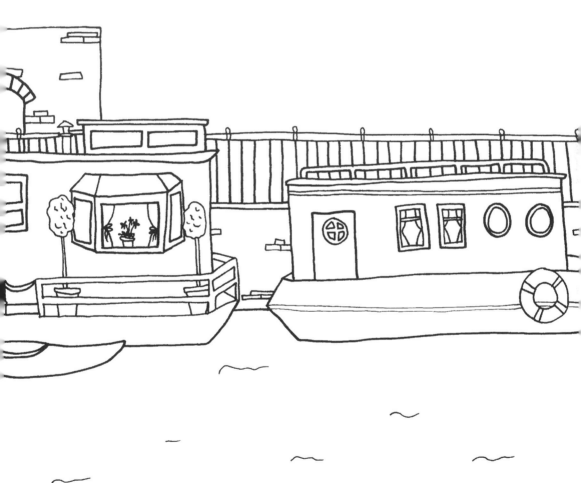

KITSCH & ART

Take a picture of the ugliest souvenirs you encounter and add the photographs to this page. Or draw them. Our favourite: the prickly sweater with the queen's dog.

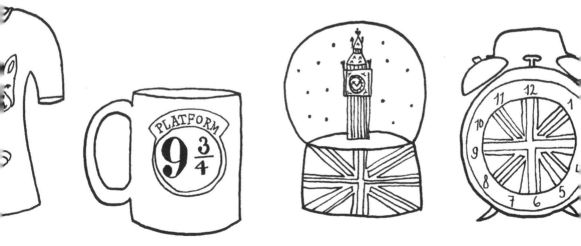

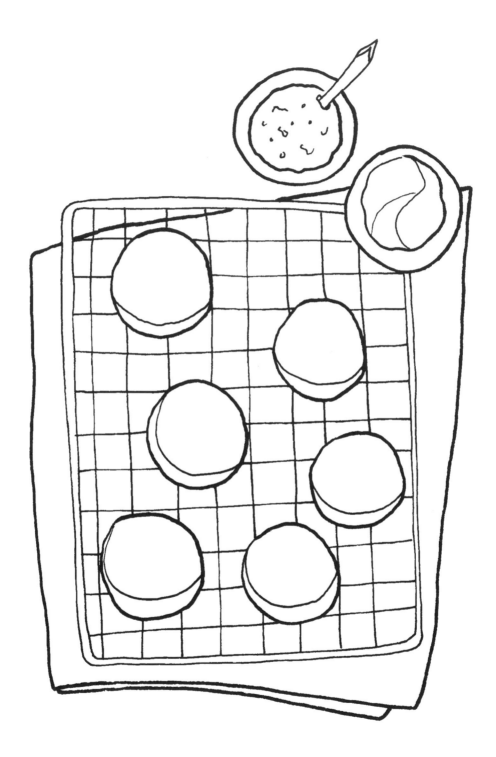

SCONES

Scones and clotted cream, with a tuft of jam. Nearly just as easy as baking muffins!

500 gr. fine flour
2 packets of baking powder
½ tsp salt
50 gr. sugar
2 tbsp vanilla sugar
125 gr. cold butter, in cubes
250 ml milk, warm juice from ½ lemon
whisked egg for glazing

EXTRA
round biscuit cutters (Ø 5 cm)
baking paper

Preheat the oven with 1 baking tray inside at 220 °C. Mix the flour, baking powder, salt, sugar and vanilla sugar in a bowl. Add the cold butter, and roll everything between your fingertips until rough, dry grains emerge. Make a dent in the mixture, pour in the warm milk and the lemon juice and knead rapidly into a dough (it remains fairly moist). Cover your worktop with flour. Lower the dough onto the worktop and knead it into a thick slab of approx. 3 cm thick. Cut out round pieces with a diameter of approx. 5 cm - use up all the dough, and if necessary, knead leftovers together into another thick slab. Glaze the round chunks with whisked egg. Place a sheet of baking paper on the baking tray, place the scones on top with 3 cm space between them and bake them until they have a golden yellow colour in approx. 10 minutes.
Let them cool on a shelf and store in an airtight and closed-off container. Serve with cream and tasty jam.

MY 8 MOST BEAUTIFUL PHOTOS

Print out on 5 x 5 cm stick them in.
Just like a real Polaroid!

BARGAINS & BAD BUYS

Regretting that one jacket you left
behind? If only you could have
just kept yourself from buying
those expensive trousers.
Draw your bad buys, bargains and
missed purchases here.

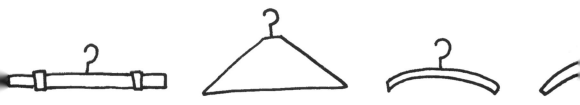

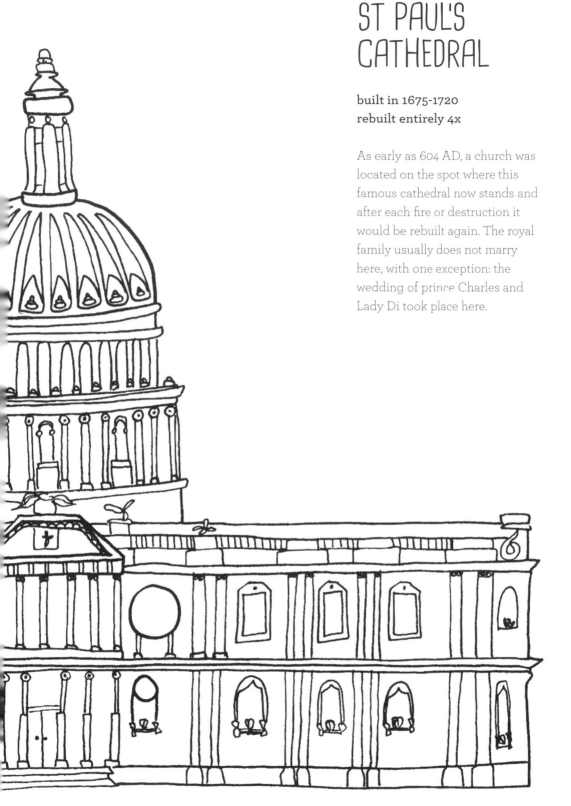

ST PAUL'S CATHEDRAL

built in 1675-1720
rebuilt entirely 4x

As early as 604 AD, a church was located on the spot where this famous cathedral now stands and after each fire or destruction it would be rebuilt again. The royal family usually does not marry here, with one exception: the wedding of prince Charles and Lady Di took place here.

ROOM WITH A VIEW

What do you see when you look
out the window: trees in the park,
Buckingham Palace, the Tower
Bridge?
Draw the view from your hotel
room here.

AT THE CHEF'S TABLE

Only in London: dining in one of the restaurants from well-known TV chefs. Reserve a table at on of the addresses below and draw your dish on this page.

☐ **OTTOLENGHI**
 Multiple restaurants across the city
 www.ottolenghi.co.uk

☐ **JAMIE OLIVER**
 Multiple restaurants across the city
 www.jamieoliver.com

☐ **GORDON RAMSAY**
 Multiple restaurants across the city
 www.gordonramsay.com

☐ **DINNER BY HESTON BLUMENTHAL**
 Mandarin Oriental Hyde Park
 66 Knightsbridge
 London SW1X 7LA
 www.dinnerbyheston.com

☐ **GRANGER & CO BY BILL GRANGER**
 Multiple restaurants across the city
 www.grangerandco.com

☐ ....

☐ ....

☐ ....

Nº1
Nº1
PIMM'S
THE ORIGINAL NO1 CUP
Nº1
PRODUCED
IN
GREAT BRITAIN

PIMM'S

Forget hip cocktails or the summer drink hit of the year so and so. For years, Pimm's has been a hit in the UK and with good reason. Pimm's No.1 Cup is a refreshing herbal liqueur with a hint of lemon.

⅓ parts Pimm's liqueur
⅔ parts sparkling lemonade
slices of lemon
slices of lime strawberries
half a cucumber sliced
leaves from a few sprigs of mint
ice cubes

Fill ¾ of a large decanter with Pimm's and tasty lemonade. Add some fruit and finish with ice cubes. You can also prepare the Pimm's in this manner for a glass.

COME IN, WE'RE OPEN

How many department stores can you handle during your trip to London? The best-known ones are Harrods and Harvey Nichols, but make sure not to miss out on Marks & Spencer, Liberty, Fortnum & Mason, John Lewis and Selfridges. The stuff you buy there will undoubtedly be splendid, but their bags are also well worth your while.

TATE MODERN

Most-visited gallery in the world: nearly 5 million visitors per year.

The Tate Modern, one of the most beautiful galleries we know, displays modern art from 1900 and onwards. It is located in the old Bankside Power Station, which was rendered obsolete in 1981, and was reopened in 2000 as a gallery. In the winter, the Turbine Hall offers large, impressive exhibitions by international artists. In addition to the alternating exhibitions there is also a permanent collection.

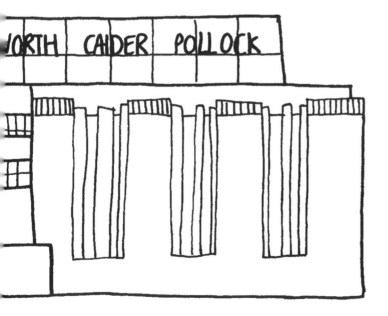

OVER THE LONDON ROOFTOPS

Draw the view from Tower Bridge,
Primrose Hill, the London Eye or
the roof terrace of a restaurant.

BLAH-BLAH-BLAH

On her new lover. About his boss. On the annoying children. About her new coat, which is truly hideous. Have you heard about so and so yet, who is doing this and that?
Record them, those shameless conversations. Or only note down the most beautiful quotes.

Inspiration for at home, at work, on holidays, the rest of my life

TYPICAL LONDON

Print out your photographs on 5 x 5 cm and glue them in here. Just like a real Polaroid!

GALLERY OF THE GREATS

Visited the National Portrait Gallery on St. Martin's Place yet? In the museum you'll find 200,000 portraits of famous and less famous Brits, which have been collected since 1856. Copy a few of those faces in a drawing. Or draw your own celebrities.

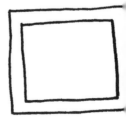

GIN & TONIC

If you are planning to drink a G&T, then do it in London. Even if it's just for the pretty labels. Out of the dozens of old distilleries in the city only few remain, but in recent years many new, small distilleries have been opened. *Cheers, mate*!

ALWAYS SOMETHING TO CELEBRATE

The English flag is always flying somewhere and this flag line instantly makes us cheerful. We've left plenty of room below it for you to draw something festive: the birth of new prince, horse races at Ascot, the boat race on the Thames, street food market...

18 PAIRS OF GLASSES, BEARDS, BUNS, TURBANS, SUMMER FRECKLES & MOHAWKS GET CREATIVE!